Early TRANSPORTATION Encyclopedias

TRACTORS

by Brenda Scott Royce

Early Encyclopedias

An Imprint of Abdo Reference

abdobooks.com

abdobooks.com

Published by Abdo Reference, a division of ABDO, PO Box 398166, Minneapolis, Minnesota 55439.

Printed in China
102023
012024

THIS BOOK CONTAINS
RECYCLED MATERIALS

Editor: Carrie Hasler
Series Designer: Candice Keimig

Library of Congress Control Number: 2023939671

Publisher's Cataloging-in-Publication Data

Names: Royce, Brenda Scott, author.
Title: Tractors / by Brenda Scott Royce
Description: Minneapolis, Minnesota : Abdo Reference, 2024 | Series: Early transportation encyclopedias | Includes online resources and index.
Identifiers: ISBN 9781098292942 (lib. bdg.) | ISBN 9798384910886 (ebook)
Subjects: LCSH: Tractors--Juvenile literature. | Farm equipment--Juvenile literature. | Machinery--Juvenile literature. | Vehicles--Juvenile literature. | Transportation--Juvenile literature. | Encyclopedias and dictionaries--Juvenile literature.
Classification: DDC 629.224--dc23

CONTENTS

Let's Plow Ahead!

Tractors are mighty machines. They help on farms. Farmers use tractors to prepare soil, plant seeds, and harvest crops. They use them to pull, push, or lift heavy loads.

FUN FACT!

Tractors changed farming. Today, they are used all around the world!

Early tractors were big. They were expensive. Not many farmers could buy one. Then Henry Ford made the Fordson Model F. It was a small tractor. It was cheap. It became very popular!

Did You Know?

Before tractors, most farmers used horses, mules, and oxen. But a tractor is stronger than an animal. It can pull a plow faster. It doesn't need to eat or rest.

How Tractors Work

A mix of gas and air enters the engine. This gives the engine power. Power goes to the tractor's transmission. The transmission turns the wheels or tracks. Tractors are slow. They are built for power, not speed.

Did You Know?

Implements are special tools. They are attached to tractors. They are powered by a shaft called a power take-off (PTO).

Control levers: move the tractor forward or backward
Exhaust pipe: where engine fumes come out
Steering wheel: moves the tractor left or right
Engine: powers the tractor
Wheel: rolls the tractor

TIMELINE

1890s: The first steam plows were used on American farms.

1892: John Froelich invented a gasoline-powered tractor.

1907: The Hart-Parr Company began to use the word *tractor*.

1919: International Harvester sold the first tractor with PTO.

1919: The Nebraska Tractor Law said tractors have to be tested before they are sold.

1932: Rubber tires began to replace steel wheels on tractors.

1954: Tractors outnumbered horses and mules on American farms.

1976: All tractors had to have rollover bars for driver safety.

1979: Thousands of farmers drove tractors to Washington, DC. They wanted better farming laws.

1987: The first crawlers with rubber tracks were sold.

1996: The first tractors with Global Positioning System (GPS) were sold.

Farms grow food. Farmers use tractors every step of the way.

Getting Ready

Tractors help get the soil ready for planting. Sharp blades break up the ground. The soil becomes soft. It's ready for planting!

Planting Seeds

Tractors use machines to drop seeds into the soil. The seeds are spaced out. They have room to grow.

Tending Plants

Tractors spread fertilizer on crops. Fertilizer helps them grow. Tractors spray pesticides. This keeps bugs away. Tractors can also help remove weeds.

Harvest Time

When crops are ripe, it's time to gather them. Giant tractors help. A harvester can pick several rows of vegetables at once.

Most tractors today run on gasoline or diesel. Some run on biodiesel or methane. But the first tractors ran on steam.

Best Steam Tractor

This steam tractor was built by Daniel Best Agricultural Works. Steam engines work by burning wood or oil to boil water. The boiling water makes steam. The steam makes pressure that powers the tractor.

FUN FACT!

J. I. Case and Company made the first steam engine tractor in 1869.

It took three people to operate this huge tractor. One person sat in the driver's seat. Another person stoked the fire. The third person controlled the brakes.

Year Made:	**Weight:**	**Length:**	**Height:**
1903	More than 36,000 pounds (16,329 kg)	28 feet (8.5 m)	17 feet, 4 inches (5.3 m)

Did You Know?

The tank on the Best steam tractor held 940 gallons (3,558 l) of water which was boiled into steam. The large tractor required a lot of steam to run.

Bulldog

The Bulldog was made by the Lanz tractor company. It could run on many types of fuel—even vegetable oil! The first Bulldog tractors didn't have a cooling system. So, they didn't work well in hot climates. The Bulldog was still a popular tractor. More than 220,000 were sold.

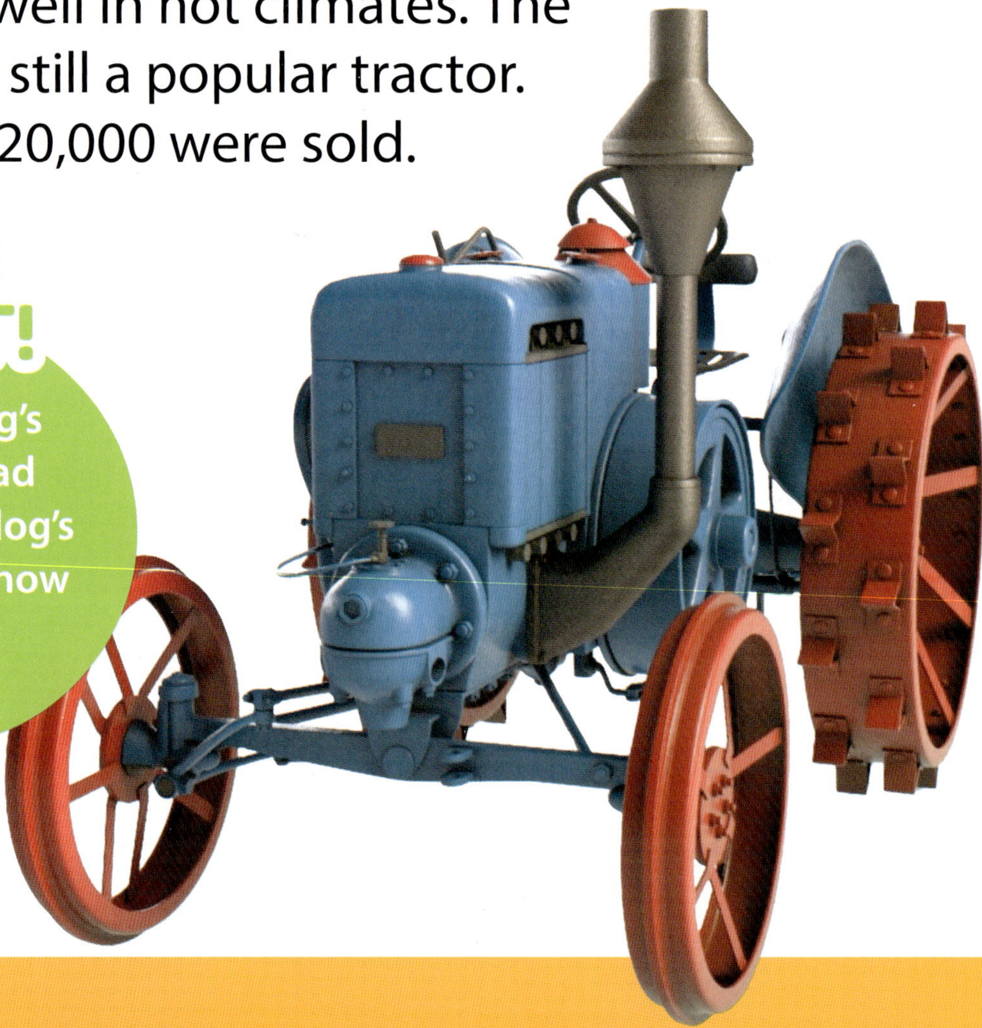

FUN FACT!

The Bulldog's engine head looks like a dog's nose. That's how it got its name!

Years Made:
1921 to 1960

Weight:
About 4,000 pounds
(1,814 kg)

Length:
About 9 feet
(2.7 m)

Height:
About 7 feet
(2.1 m)

Did You Know?

This tractor's steering wheel was removable. It had two jobs. First, it was used to start the engine. Then it went back in place to steer the tractor.

Comfortractor

Meet the Minneapolis-Moline UDLX! It's nickname was the "Comfortractor." It was a tractor that looked like a car. It was meant to be a blend of both. It could plow fields and drive on roads.

The Comfortractor had an enclosed cab. It was one of the first tractors to have one. Inside, there was a radio and a heater. Those were rare back then.

Years Made:
1938 to 1941

Weight:
6,400 pounds
(2,903 kg)

Length:
11 feet, 9 inches
(3.6 m)

Height:
7 feet, 10 inches
(2.4 m)

Did You Know?
The Comfortractor had headlights. It was designed for farming at night.

The Comfortractor was a flop. It was expensive. Farmers didn't want to spend that much money.

FUN FACT!

Only about 100 Comfortractors were sold.

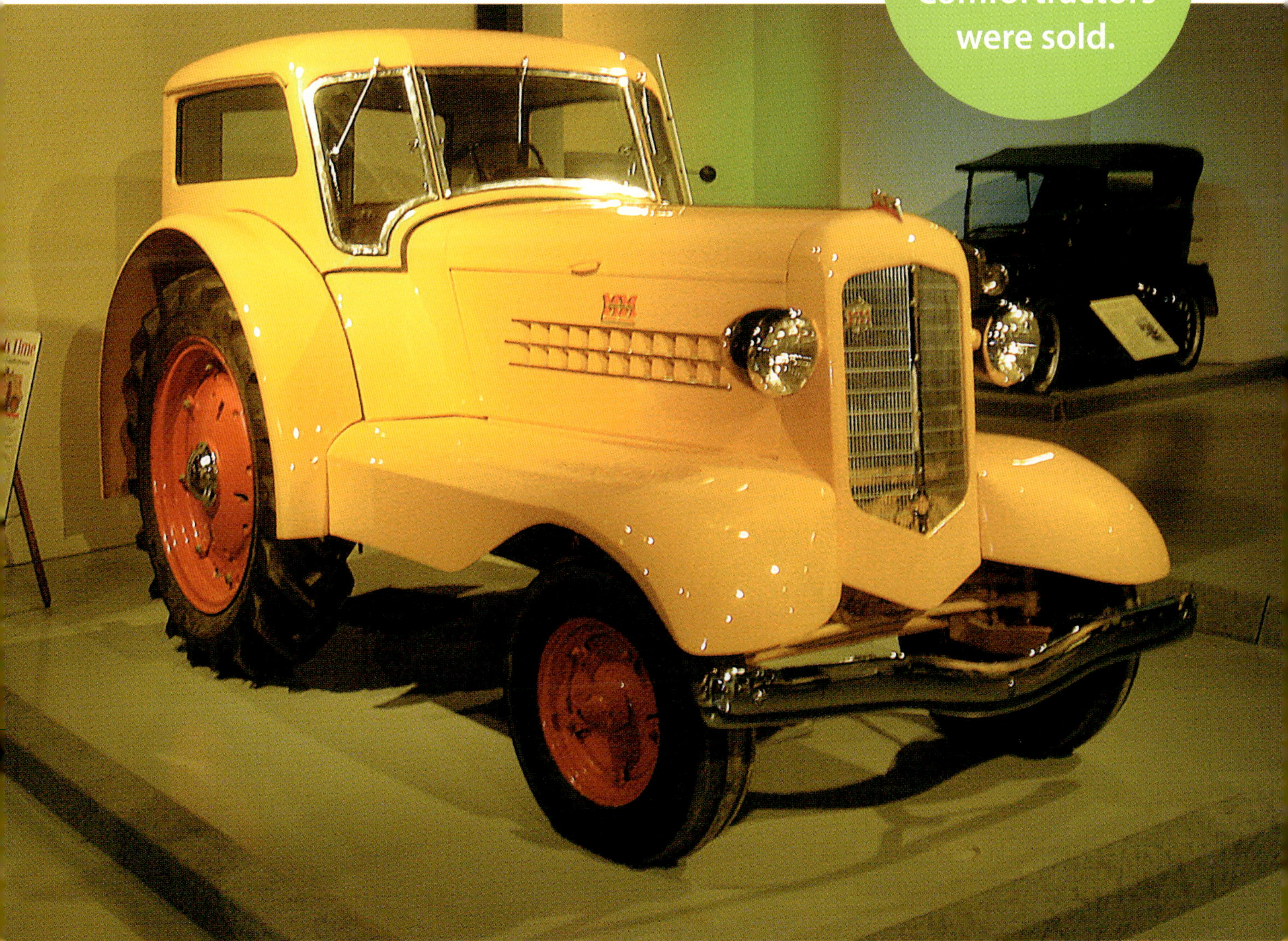

Fordson Model F

The Model F was built by Henry Ford. He started the Ford Motor Company in 1903. He built cars that people could afford. He wanted to do the same thing with tractors.

FUN FACT!

The Model F was small. It had a low price.

Ford began making tractors. In 1917, he created a new company with his son. *Fordson* is short for "Ford and son."

Years Made:
1917 to 1928

Weight:
2,500 pounds
(1,134 kg)

Length:
8 feet, 6 inches
(2.6 m)

Height:
4 feet, 7 inches
(1.4 m)

Did You Know?

The Fordson was the best-selling tractor during the years it was made. It is also one of the best-selling tractors of all time.

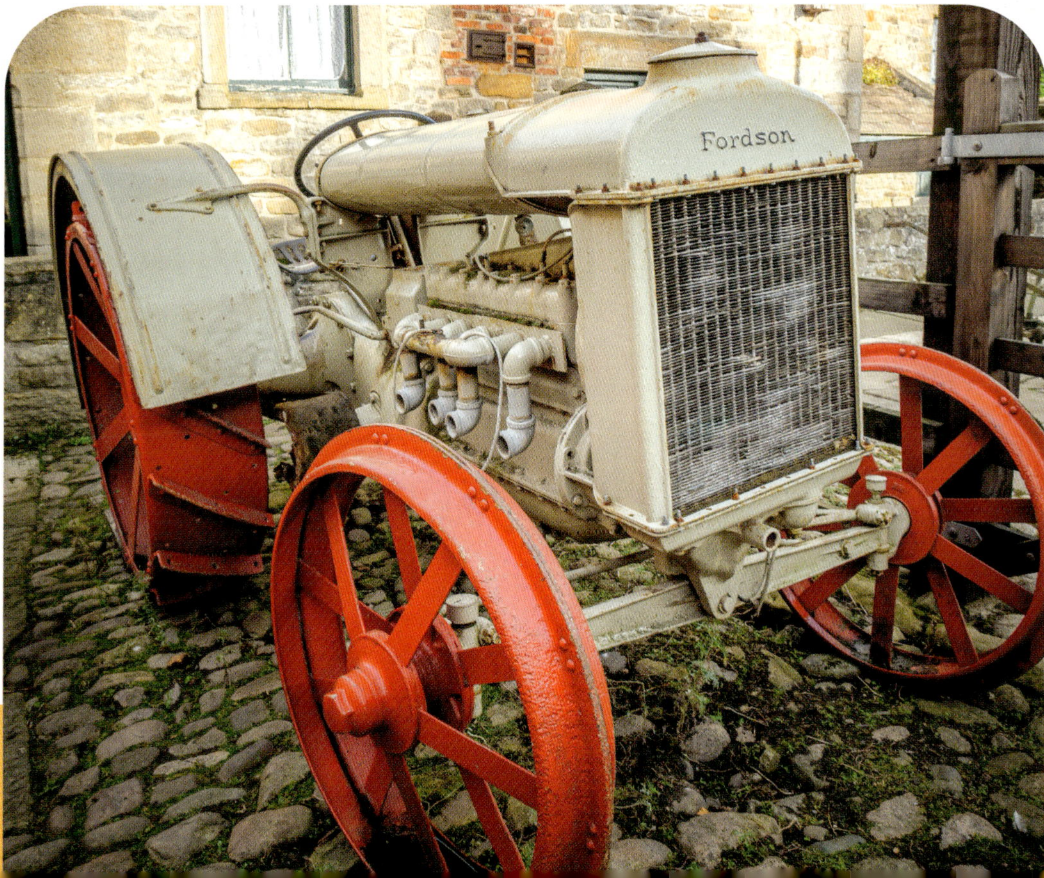

Gray Drum Drive

The Drum Drive was made by the Gray Tractor Company. There were no back wheels. Instead, there was a single hollow drum. The tractor looked like a large roller. It smoothed soil without packing it hard. A metal cover kept the engine dry. This also gave the tractor its odd look.

The driver's seat was behind the engine. It was hard to see the field ahead. To get a better view, the driver had to stand up or swing the seat out to one side.

Years Made:
1914 to 1933

Weight:
6,200 pounds
(2,812 kg)

Length:
14 feet, 6 inches
(4.4 m)

Height:
5 feet, 6 inches
(1.7 m)

FUN FACT!
This tractor's top speed was just a little more than 3 miles per hour (5 kmh).

Little Bull

This tractor looked like a lopsided tricycle. One of its rear wheels was much larger than the other. At first, the tractor sold well.

But the Little Bull had big problems. The driver couldn't see which way the front wheel was turned. A large arrow on top pointed the way. The tractor was also wobbly. It was weak. It could not pull a heavy plow. Many buyers were unhappy.

Years Made:	**Weight:**	**Length:**	**Height:**
1913 to 1918	2,900 pounds (1,315 kg)	About 10 feet (3 m)	5 feet (1.5 m)

Little Grey Fergie

The Ferguson TE-20 was a small farm tractor. Its nickname was "Little Grey Fergie." It was designed by Harry Ferguson. He was a mechanic and an inventor. He grew up on a farm in Ireland.

FUN FACT!

TE-20 **stands for "Tractor, England, 20 horsepower."**

Three-point hitch on the TE-20

Ferguson invented the three-point hitch. This changed the way tractors use tools. Older tractors dragged equipment across the ground. The three-point hitch connected tools in a better way. This made tractors safer. Most tractors use this hitch today.

Years Made:	Weight:	Length:	Height:
1946 to 1948	2,760 pounds (1,252 kg)	9 feet, 7 inches (2.9 m)	4 feet, 4 inches (1.3 m)

Did You Know?

Explorer Sir Edmund Hillary went to the South Pole in 1957. He brought five of these tractors with him. They were painted red. This made them easier to see in the snow!

Old Reliable

Charles Hart and Charles Parr met in college. They created a company. Together they built a gas-powered engine called the Hart-Parr 30-60. They used the word *tractor* in their ads.

"Old Reliable" was the nickname for the 30-60. The tractor was strong. Most of its parts were made of steel. It weighed more than 10 tons (9.07 metric tons). That's heavier than an elephant!

Years Made:
1907 to 1918

Weight:
20,100 pounds
(9,117 kg)

Length:
16 feet, 8 inches
(5.1 m)

Height:
12 feet, 4 inches
(3.8 m)

Did You Know?

Before tractors got their name, they had other names:

- traction engine
- agricultural motor
- agrimotor
- automotive plow

FUN FACT!

The word *tractor* combines "traction" and "motor."

Waterloo Boy Model N

The Waterloo Boy was created by the Waterloo Gasoline Engine Company. It was built in Waterloo, Iowa. The John Deere Company bought the company in 1918.

The Waterloo Boy did not use gas. It used a fuel called kerosene. Kerosene costs less than gas. This made the Waterloo Boy cheaper to run.

Years Made:
1916 to 1923

Weight:
6,183 pounds
(2,805 kg)

Length:
11 feet
(3.4 m)

Height:
5 feet, 3 inches
(1.6 m)

FUN FACT!

Today, John Deere is one of the world's top tractor makers.

Did You Know?

Model N was the first tractor sold by John Deere.

JOHN DEERE & COMPANY

John Deere is a famous tractor company. But they started out selling plows and other farming tools.

John Deere was born in Vermont in 1804. He became a blacksmith. He moved to Illinois. Farmers there had a big problem. Thick soil stuck to their plows. They had to stop every few minutes to scrape off the mud.

FUN FACT!

John Deere construction vehicles are painted yellow.

Deere took steel from a broken saw. He turned it into a plow blade. He polished and shaped the blade. The soil didn't stick. He sold the plow and made many more. His company grew. Deere died in 1886. Thirty-two years later, his company began selling tractors.

Did You Know?

Most John Deere tractors are painted green with yellow trim. The company's logo features a leaping deer.

COMBINE HARVESTERS

Combine harvesters have two jobs. They harvest, and they thresh. Harvesting is cutting and gathering crops. Threshing separates grain from stalks.

People used to do these jobs. Combines speed up farming. They can harvest many crop rows at once.

wheat harvester

Combines have headers in front. Different crops need different headers. A wheat harvester has blades. The blades rotate. They cut the wheat.

FUN FACT!

The character named Frank in the movie *Cars* is a combine harvester.

combine header

Claas Lexion 8900

The Claas Lexion 8900 is one of the world's largest combines. It makes harvesting large fields take less time. This combine's header is so wide, it's like pushing a bus sideways!

Did You Know?

The Claas Lexion 8900 is too wide to drive down a road. The header must be taken off first.

Years Made:
2019 to present

Weight:
more than 22 tons
(20 metric tons)

Width of Header:
45 feet
(13.7 m)

Corn Harvesters

A corn combine has metal points in front. They look like teeth! The more points, the more rows it can harvest at the same time.

The points go between rows of corn stalks. The stalks are guided into the cutter.

The combine strips off the stalks of each plant. The leaves are stripped off too. Then it removes the kernels.

FUN FACT!

Iowa produces more corn than any other state.

Wheat Harvesters

Wheat is used to make bread, cereal, and pasta. But only the grains are used. The harvester separates them from the rest of the wheat plant.

Did You Know?

About 49 million tons (44.5 million metric tons) of wheat are grown in the United States each year.

The grain shoots out of a long tube. A tractor or truck drives next to the harvester. It collects the grain.

The stems are left in the field. They are also called stalks. Dried stalks turn into straw. Straw is used as bedding for animals.

FUN FACT!

People have been growing wheat for 10,000 years!

OTHER COMBINE HARVESTERS

New Holland Braud Grape Harvester

This harvester shakes grape vines. It collects bunches of grapes. Next, it removes the stems. Then it cleans the grapes.

Sampo Rosenlew 2050

The Sampo 2050 can be used to harvest oats.

Yanmar CA315

The small Yanmar CA315 combine can harvest rice.

COMPACT TRACTORS

Compact tractors may be short or skinny. They are built for tight spaces and light loads. They perform many jobs on a farm. They can be used to lift or move things. They can help dig holes. They can help with harvests.

Did You Know?

Tractor loads can be heavy. Weights can help to balance the load. A weight mounted to the front or back of a tractor keeps it from tipping.

A compact tractor fits inside a barn or building. It delivers food to farm animals. It may also be used to clean out stalls.

Fendt Vario 200V

The Fendt Vario 200V is a vineyard tractor. The *V* stands for "vineyard." A vineyard is a farm that grows only grapes.

Vineyard tractors are narrow. The Fendt Vario is just 3.5 feet (1.1 m) wide. It can drive between rows of grapevines easily.

Years Made:
2017 to 2021

Weight:
6,305 pounds
(2,860 kg)

Length:
11 feet, 10 inches
(3.6 m)

Height:
7 feet, 10 inches
(2.4 m)

FUN FACT!
California grows more grapes than any other state.

John Deere 2038R

Compact tractors, like the John Deere 2038R, can squeeze between trees in a forest. It can be used to gather logs.

Some tractors don't have a cab. Instead, they have a thick metal bar over the driver's seat called the ROPS. It stands for "rollover protection structure." It protects the driver if the tractor tips over.

Years Made:
2017 to present

Weight:
2,436 pounds
(1,105 kg)

Length:
9 feet, 6 inches
(2.9 m)

Height:
7 feet, 7 inches
(2.3 m)

JOHN DEERE
KRPAN
3,5 E
KRPAN 3.5E

McCormick-Deering O-6

This tractor was used in an orchard. Orchard tractors drive between rows of trees. They help workers take care of trees and pick fruit.

A smooth shield covers the back wheels. The shield protects the tractor and the fruit. The tractor won't snag tree branches as it drives past.

FUN FACT!

An orchard grows fruit trees, such as apples or oranges.

Years Made:
1940 to 1953

Weight:
5,310 pounds
(2,409 kg)

Length:
11 feet, 10 inches
(3.6 m)

Height:
5 feet, 3 inches
(1.6 m)

Shibaura ST324

Compact tractors can be used in parks and golf courses. They help workers take care of these areas.

Tread is the pattern of ridges and grooves on a tire. The Shibaura's tires have smooth tread. They are gentle on lawns. They don't dig up the ground.

Some tractors have large ridges. They are good for driving on rough ground. They help tractors pull plows and other tools.

Years Made:
2001 to 2017

Weight:
1,640 pounds
(744 kg)

Length:
9 feet
(2.7 m)

Height:
7 feet, 6 inches
(2.3 m)

FUN FACT!
Tractors with large ridges grip the soil better.

TONS OF FUN

Tractors are made for work, but they are also fun! People of all ages love tractors.

Old tractors are popular in parades.

Diggerland USA is an amusement park in New Jersey. They have construction and tractor-themed rides.

Diggerland USA

tractors on display

Owners show off their tractors at fairs and festivals. Some shows feature "dancing" tractors.

dancing tractors

CRAWLERS

A crawler, like the Case IH Magnum 380 Rowtrac, has tracks instead of tires. The tracks are wrapped around a set of wheels. As the wheels turn, they move the track forward. Tracks spread the tractor's weight across a larger surface.

Tracks have better grip than wheels. Crawlers can climb steep hills. They can drive on muddy fields or sandy beaches. The tracks keep the crawler from slipping or sinking.

Case IH Magnum 380 Rowtrac

Years Made:
2015 to present

Weight:
37,728 pounds
(17,113 kg)

Length:
20 feet, 9 inches
(6.3 m)

Height:
11 feet, 4 inches
(3.5 m)

FUN FACT!

A half-track tractor has tires in front and tracks in back.

Caterpillar Challenger MT765C

In 1904, Benjamin Holt built the first working crawler. Someone thought it moved like a caterpillar. "Caterpillar" became the nickname for crawlers. In 1925, Holt started the Caterpillar Tractor Company.

FUN FACT!

No flats! Unlike a tire, a rubber track can't be punctured.

The first Caterpillar Challenger was built in 1987. It was the first successful crawler with rubber tracks. The MT765C is a newer version.

Rubber tracks are quieter than metal tracks. They are also gentler on surfaces. Steel wires inside the rubber tracks make them extra strong.

Years Made:
2009 to 2011

Weight:
31,075 pounds
(14,095 kg)

Length:
19 feet, 5 inches
(5.9 m)

Height:
11 feet, 4 inches
(3.5 m)

International Harvester BTD-6

Crawlers are used mostly on uneven or rough ground. This makes it risky for the driver. The tractor could tip or roll over. Early crawlers did not have a cabin. Crawlers today have built-in cabins or roll bars to protect the driver.

This tractor didn't have a steering wheel. Instead, it had two levers. The right lever controlled the right track. The left lever controlled the left track. Many crawlers have this type of steering system.

Years Made:
1955 to 1975

Weight:
9,100 pounds
(4,128 kg)

Length:
8 feet, 8 inches
(2.6 m)

Height:
5 feet
(1.5 m)

INTERNATIONAL
BTD
6
DIESEL

John Deere 9620RX

This tractor is a quadtrac. *Quad* means "four." A quadtrac has four triangular tracks. The tracks help it glide over rocky surfaces and through mud or snow.

The 9620RX is heavy. But because the tractor has tracks, it doesn't press on the ground as much as if it had wheels. This is better for the soil.

Years Made:
2016 to 2021

Weight:
55,500 pounds
(25,174 kg)

Length:
26 feet, 10 inches
(8.2 m)

Height:
13 feet, 6 inches
(4.1 m)

Did You Know?

The 9620RX has a horsepower of 620 hp. This means it's powerful. Most tractors have a horsepower of 200 hp or less.

FUN FACT!

The cabin on the 9620RX sits high off the ground. This gives the drivers good visibility.

Oliver OC-6 High Crop Crawler

Early crawlers had steel tracks. They can damage roadways. Modern tractors have rubber tracks.

FUN FACT!

Steel tracks are tough but noisy.

Crawlers with steel tracks can't travel very fast. This tractor's top speed is just over 8 miles per hour (12.9 kmh).

Years Made:
1953 to 1960

Weight:
About 5,700 pounds
(2,585 kg)

Length:
10 feet, 2 inches
(3.1 m)

Height:
4 feet, 9 inches
(1.4 m)

GARDEN TRACTORS

Some of the smallest tractors aren't found on farms. These small tractors are made for gardens and lawns. You may have one in your backyard.

FUN FACT!

Americans spend an average of four hours per week taking care of their lawn.

The main job of a lawn or garden tractor is to mow grass. They can help with other jobs too. Some garden tractors can tow a dump cart. A dump cart can be used to haul leaves, soil, or rocks.

Craftsman LT1500

Years Made:
2009 to 2013

Weight:
500 pounds
(227 kg)

Length:
5 feet, 10 inches
(1.8 m)

Height:
2 feet, 10 inches
(0.9 m)

A riding lawn mower is a type of garden tractor. It is also called a ride-on mower. Sometimes it's called a lawn tractor. It can mow a lawn faster than a push mower.

Cub Cadet 127

Years Made:
1969 to 1971

Weight:
650 pounds
(295 kg)

Length:
5 feet, 4 inches
(1.6 m)

Height:
3 feet, 4 inches
(1 m)

FUN FACT!
The Cub Cadet was one of the first lawn tractors.

Did You Know?

Lawn mower racing is a popular sport. The blades are removed. This keeps people safe!

Ford LGT-16D

You can tell a lot about this tractor from its model number. *LGT* stands for "Lawn and Garden Tractor." The number 16 is the tractor's horsepower. *D* stands for "diesel."

Years Made:
1989 to 1991

Weight:
815 pounds
(370 kg)

Length:
5 feet, 11 inches
(1.8 m)

Height:
3 feet, 6 inches
(1.1 m)

FUN FACT!
Special attachments can turn a garden tractor into a snow blower.

Grillo FD 13.09

The Grillo FD 13.09 is a lawn mower that is built to cut and collect grass. It is mostly used to take care of grass at schools, parks, sports facilities, campgrounds, and other places with large lawns.

The Grillo has its blades in the front. This means it can mow under trees and bushes. A mower deck covers the blades.

Some garden tractors have grass catchers. The grass catcher is attached in back.

Years Made:
2014 to present

Weight:
2,711 pounds
(1,230 kg)

Length:
10 feet, 8 inches
(3.3 m)

Height:
5 feet, 8 inches
(1.7 m)

FUN FACT!
Grass catchers collect cut grass.

Husqvarna TC 138 Garden Tractor

Big Bud 747

The Big Bud 747 tractor was one of a kind. Other Big Buds have been built, but the 747 was the largest. It was specially made for a cotton farm in California.

Year Made:
1978

Weight:
About 100,000 pounds
(45,359 kg)

Length:
About 29 feet
(8.8 m)

Height:
14 feet
(4.3 m)

FUN FACT!

Big Bud has eight tires. Each tire is 7 feet (2.1 m) tall!

JCB Fastrac 8330

The JCB Fastrac is the world's fastest tractor. Motorcycle racer Guy Martin turned a Fastrac into a racing tractor. He drove it at more than 135 miles per hour (217 kmh)! That's a world record.

Years Made:
2016 to present

Weight:
24,450 pounds
(11,090 kg)

Length:
18 feet, 6 inches
(5.6 m)

Height:
11 feet, 1 inch
(3.4 m)

IMPLEMENT CARRIERS

Tractors and tools were meant to go together. A tractor alone is a powerful vehicle. A tractor with a tool can do much more.

A tractor's tools are called implements. They are also called attachments. Why? They are attached to the tractor.

Did You Know?
Implements can go on the front or back of a tractor.

Most tractor tools can be taken on and off. Different tools do different jobs. A farmer may have many tools and just one tractor. The same tractor can be used for different jobs. It can plow a field one day. It can plant seeds the next day. The tractor can spray crops. It can trim hedges.

FUN FACT!

Implements are attached to a drawbar on the tractor.

Balers

A baler collects loose hay or straw. Then it presses it into a bale. *Bale* is another word for *bundle*.

Did You Know?

Hay and straw look alike. Hay is a type of grass that has been cut and dried. It has vitamins and minerals. Many farm animals eat hay.

Straw is the hollow stem of wheat and other grain plants. When these plants are harvested, the stems are left behind. When the stems dry, they become straw. Straw has many uses on a farm. But it is not food. Many farm animals sleep on straw.

FUN FACT!

A bale wrapper wraps bales in plastic to keep them dry.

Cultivators and Harrows

Cultivators prepare the soil for planting. First, a plow breaks up hard ground. Then a cultivator mixes the dirt. Cultivators also dig up weeds.

Did You Know?

The sharp points on a cultivator are called tines.

A harrow is a type of cultivator. A disc harrow has round metal discs. They are in rows. The discs slice through clumps of soil.

FUN FACT!

A set of discs is called a gang.

Hay Turners and Rakes

After hay is cut, it is left to dry in the sun. A hay turner flips the hay and spreads it out. This helps it dry faster.

A hay rake turns the hay again. It forms long piles called windrows. The hay dries completely. Then it is baled.

FUN FACT!

A hay turner is also called a tedder.

Planters and Seeders

Planters drop seeds into the soil. Many rows are planted at once. Seeds are dropped out in perfectly spaced rows.

A seed drill buries seeds. First, it drills a row of holes. Seeds fall in. Then the seed drill covers the seeds with soil.

Did You Know?

The seeds are held in bins called hoppers.

seed drill

Plows

Plowing is the first step in preparing fields for planting. A plow has curved metal blades. These blades cut and turn the soil. A plow can have one blade or many blades.

A furrow is a groove cut into the soil. Plows create long rows of furrows. Seeds are planted in furrows.

FUN FACT!

A push-pull plow has one plow in front and another in back.

Rollers and Scrapers

Rollers and scrapers help prepare a field for planting. A scraper levels the soil. Then a smoother presses rocks into the ground. This makes it easier for tractors and combines to do their jobs.

Sprayers and Spreaders

Sprayers have wide arms with nozzles. Sprayers water crops. They can also spray chemicals to kill pests and weeds. Spreaders spread fertilizer over crops.

FUN FACT!

A muck spreader spreads animal manure. This is used as fertilizer.

ROW CROP TRACTORS

Many crops, like corn and potatoes, are grown in rows. To tend these plants, farmers drive up and down every row. A row crop tractor is just right for the job. Its wheels fit in the rows.

The tractor drives down one row. When it reaches the end, it turns around. These tractors can make tight turns.

FUN FACT!

Row crops are replanted every year.

Allis Chalmers Model B

The Model B was built to pass over taller plants. The tractor's front axle was arched. This prevented the plants from being damaged as the tractor drove over them.

Some row crop tractors were made for specific crops. The Model B had a Potato Special. It had a narrow track, which helped it fit down rows of potatoes. There also was an Asparagus Special. It had a higher clearance than other Model Bs to move over asparagus plants.

Years Made:
1938 to 1957

Weight:
2,060 pounds
(934 kg)

Length:
9 feet
(2.7 m)

Height:
6 feet, 5 inches
(2 m)

FUN FACT!

Allis Chalmers tractors are painted orange. The color was inspired by poppies.

Ford 4000

The Ford 4000 came in different models. Some were built with one wheel in front, like a tricycle. These models were best for cultivating crops grown in rows. One wheel in front also allowed the tractors to make tight turns.

Some Ford 4000s had two small wheels in front. They were used as row crop tractors too. But they could also be used for other jobs on the farm.

Years Made:
1962 to 1975

Weight:
4,885 pounds
(2,216 kg)

Length:
11 feet, 4 inches
(3.5 m)

Height:
About 5 feet
(1.5 m)

FUN FACT!

Tractors with four wheels are more stable than tractors with three.

International Harvester Farmall M

One of the first row crop tractors was made by International Harvester. The Farmall got its name because it can farm all kinds of crops.

These tractors are bright red. This color makes them stand out in a field of green crops.

Years Made:
1939 to 1954

Weight:
4,858 pounds
(2,204 kg)

Length:
11 feet
(3.4 m)

Height:
6 feet, 5 inches
(2 m)

FUN FACT!
Many people like to buy and restore Farmall M tractors.

J. I. Case High Crop

High crop tractors are a type of row crop tractor. The J. I. Case High Crop is like a tractor on stilts. Fewer than 100 of these tractors were made.

A high crop's body sits high above the ground. It can drive over tall crops and won't damage them.

Years Made:
1955 to 1957

Weight:
6,000 pounds
(2,722 kg)

Length:
11 feet, 1 inch
(3.4 m)

Height:
5 feet, 2 inches
(1.6 m)

FUN FACT!
Sugarcane is a type of tall crop.

John Deere Model A

The John Deere Model A had overhead steering. The steering shaft ran over the hood. The shaft controlled which way the wheels turned. On modern tractors, the steering shaft is hidden. It is inside the tractor's body.

1947 Model A

1935 Model A

The round wheel on the side is a flywheel. It stores energy. To start the engine, the driver spins the flywheel.

Years Made:
1934 to 1952

Weight:
3,783 pounds
(1,716 kg)

Length:
About 10 feet
(3 m)

Height:
5 feet
(1.5 m)

FUN FACT!

The Model A's nickname is "Johnny Popper." Its engine makes a popping noise.

PULLING POWER

Tractor pulling is a popular sport. It started a long time ago. Farmers would compete to see who had the strongest tractor. Each tractor would drag a heavy object. Whoever pulled it the farthest was the winner.

Did You Know?

A tractor pull can be very noisy . . . and messy! Wheels kick up dust and soil.

FUN FACT!
A tiebreaker is called a "pull-off."

Today, tractor pulls draw big crowds. Tractors tow a pull sled. The sled gets heavier as it is pulled. Most tracks are 320 feet (97.5 m) long. If a tractor makes it to the end of the track, it's called a "full pull."

SELF-DRIVING & TRACTOR TECHNOLOGY

Computers have changed farming. They plan tractor routes. They track where seeds are planted and monitor their growth.

Touch screens allow tractor drivers to view information about crops, weather, and more. Modern tractors have GPS receivers. GPS uses satellites in the sky to guide tractors as they drive.

FUN FACT!

The nickname for the John Deere GPS receiver is "green eggs and ham."

Drones fly above a farm. They help farmers monitor crops. Some drones spray pesticides or fertilizers.

Can a tractor drive itself? Yes! Early robotic tractors did not work well. Technology keeps improving. People are coming up with new ideas. Today, more self-driving tractors are being made.

Belarus 3523i

Year Made: 2021

This is a demo tractor. It was built in 2021. It is not for sale. It has no cab. It is controlled by cameras, sensors, and a computer.

John Deere Autonomous 8R Tractor

Year Made: 2023

John Deere showed off robotic tractors at a show. But they are not for sale yet. Autonomous tractors, like this one, will help farmers do work. This tractor can be controlled by a smartphone.

Did You Know?
The New Holland T7 Methane Power LNG looks like the T7 that runs on diesel.

New Holland T7 Methane Power LNG

Tractor makers are always coming up with new ideas. The New Holland T7 Methane Power LNG is powered by cow manure! LNG stands for "liquefied natural gas." In this case, the gas is methane. Cows produce it in their burps, farts, and manure.

Farmers mix manure with liquid into slurry. The slurry is stored in a special tank. Over time it gives off gas. The gas is pumped into the tractor's fuel tank.

Years Made:
2023 to present

FUN FACT!

Using cow manure for tractor fuel can save money. It's also good for the planet.

TWO-WHEEL TRACTORS

Agria 1700

Two-wheel tractors are also called walk-behind tractors. These tractors are used in gardens and can be found on small farms. They are used to prepare soil for planting.

FUN FACT!

The brakes on two-wheel tractors are located on the handlebars.

Did You Know?

The handlebars on the BCS 853 can swivel. They move from the front to the back of the tractor.

BCS 853

Large tractors can tow tools. So can two-wheel tractors, like the BCS 853. It can pull a tiller which works like a small plow. Two-wheel tractors can also pull planters.

Years Made:
2006 to present

Weight:
342 pounds
(155 kg)

Length:
3 feet,
10 inches
(1.2 m)

Height:
2 feet,
10 inches
(0.9 m)

OFF THE FARM

Tractors aren't used only on farms. A pushback tractor tows airplanes. These tractors are powerful. Military tractors transport troops and cargo.

Tractors can pave roads and plow snow. They help cut trees and replant forests. Construction tractors haul heavy things.

Tractors are often used to rescue people. They can drive where other vehicles can't.

FUN FACT!

A backhoe tractor is used in construction. It has a shovel and bucket.

UTILITY TRACTORS

Some tractors are built for one type of job. A utility tractor is the opposite. It can do many different jobs.

Utility tractors are larger than compact tractors. They use more attachments than row crop tractors. They are handy and hardworking.

Case IH Quantum 75C

The Case IH Quantum 75C has four-wheel drive. Tractors with four-wheel drive can do more tasks because they can get to more places.

The Quantum 75C can also handle many different tasks on a farm. Farmers can buy different attachments depending on the job. Bale spears and grips help move bales. Buckets can carry logs, soil, and other items. Grapples help move hard-to-handle material like hay. The Quantum 75C can do it all.

Years Made:
2008 to 2014

Weight:
6,140 pounds
(2,785 kg)

Length:
11 feet, 3 inches
(3.4 m)

Height:
7 feet, 4 inches
(2.2 m)

David Brown 995

The David Brown 995 came in two versions. One has a cab. The other does not. Some drivers prefer no cab. They have a better view of their fields.

David Brown 995 with cab

David Brown 995

Years Made:
1971 to 1980

Weight:
4,780 pounds
(2,168 kg)

Length:
10 feet, 6 inches
(3.2 m)

Height:
4 feet, 10 inches
(1.5 m)

FUN FACT!
A cab protects the driver from rain, wind, and dust.

Ford 600

This tractor was first made in 1954. That was a big year for tractors. There were more tractors used on American farms than horses and mules. This was the first time this happened.

The Ford 600 series had different models. Some had four-speed transmissions. Others had five-speed transmissions. Some came with a PTO and a three-point hitch. Others did not.

All of the Ford 600 tractors were popular. Many people still use them today. Others like to collect them and fix them up.

Years Made:
1954 to 1957

Weight:
3,000 pounds
(1,361 kg)

Length:
10 feet, 1 inch
(3.1 m)

Height:
4 feet, 11 inches
(1.5 m)

International Harvester 523

The International Harvester company started in 1902. Back then, they made large tractors and farm machinery. Later, they started making smaller tractors, like the 523. This tractor was durable. It was popular for smaller farms. Its large rear wheels gave it pulling power. The smaller front wheels steered.

FUN FACT!

International Harvester also made household appliances, construction equipment, and cars.

Years Made:
1965 to 1972

Weight:
5,380 pounds
(2,440 kg)

Length:
9 feet, 11 inches
(3 m)

Height:
4 feet, 11 inches
(1.5 m)

Did You Know?

International Harvester was sold in 1985 to the Case Corporation. The company is now called Case IH.

John Deere 2140

A utility tractor is sometimes called a "do all." The John Deere 2140 tractor can do many tasks. It can pull a harrow. It can pull a sprayer. It can use a hedge cutter.

Years Made:
1980 to 1987

Length:
12 feet, 11 inches
(3.9 m)

Height:
8 feet, 9 inches
(2.7 m)

Weight:
7,800 pounds
(3,538 kg)

Kubota M9000 Utility Special

Kubota is a tractor company from Japan. They made Japan's first farm tractor in 1960. Today, Kubota tractors, like the M9000, are sold around the world.

Years Made:
1997 to 2005

Weight:
5,675 pounds
(2,574 kg)

Length:
12 feet, 8 inches
(3.9 m)

Height:
8 feet, 3 inches
(2.5 m)

FUN FACT!
Kubota began selling tractors in the Unites States in 1972.

New Holland T5 Series

The New Holland T5 series has different types of transmissions. Owners can choose which kind is best for how they want to use the tractor.

The tractor's cab is built to be comfortable and quiet. It has windows all around, even on the roof. This provides good visibility. The driver can see above the tractor when using attachments like bale lifters.

Years Made:
2016 to present

Weight:
9,100 pounds
(4,128 kg)

Length:
About 16 feet
(4.9 m)

Height:
8 feet, 10 inches
(2.7 m)

Did You Know?

The New Holland tractor company did not start in Holland. It started in New Holland, Pennsylvania.

OTHER UTILITY TRACTORS

Kioti DK901C

Kioti tractors are made in South Korea. *Kioti* is said like the word *coyote*.

Did You Know?

A howling coyote is on the company's logo.

Mahindra 9500

The 9500 is a powerful tractor. It maneuvers well in tight spaces. It also has a large fuel tank. It can drive for a long time before it needs to be refueled.

FUN FACT!

Mahindra is a company from India.

Massey Ferguson 5450

Massey Ferguson tractors are known to be reliable. That means they don't break easily. They are also easy to take care of.

GLOSSARY

agricultural
Describes things that have to do with farming.

axle
A shaft for a rotating wheel or gear.

bale
A round or rectangular bundle of hay.

crop
A plant that is grown and harvested, mostly for food.

diesel
A type of fuel for tractors and other vehicles.

drawbar
A hitch where implements are attached.

durable
Able to last a long time.

four-wheel drive
A type of vehicle where all four wheels are powered by the engine.

maneuver
To move skillfully.

manure
The solid waste of domestic animals.

restore
To make something like new.

stable
Steady, not easily changed.

traction
The grip between a tractor's wheels or tracks and the ground.

transmission
The set of gears, or notched wheels, in a tractor or vehicle that help it move.

visibility
How far a person can see clearly.

TO LEARN MORE

More Books to Read

David, M. Kaye. *Tractors and Farm Machinery*. Steam Bookworks, 2021.

DK. *Total Tractor: Sticker Encyclopedia*. DK Children, 2019.

Hanáčková, Pavla. *All Aboard! Tractor*. Sky Pony Press, 2023.

Rossiter, Brienna. *Big Machines on the Farm*. North Star Editions, 2021.

Online Resources

Booklinks
NONFICTION NETWORK
FREE! ONLINE NONFICTION RESOURCES

To learn more about tractors, please visit **abdobooklinks.com** or scan this QR code. These links are routinely monitored and updated to provide the most current information available.

INDEX

PHOTO CREDITS

Cover Photos: Jorge Adriano/Shutterstock Images, front (John Deere); Sergey Kohl/Shutterstock Images, front (Lanz Bulldog); Tony Savino/Shutterstock Images, front (Case IH); watcher fox/Shutterstock Images, front (field); Gestalt Imagery/Shutterstock Images, back (crawler)

Interior Photos: Bruce Lewis/Dreamstime.com, 1, 48; Sheryl Watson/Shutterstock Images, 4, 6; Bob Pool/Shutterstock Images, 5 (top); Alexandru Logel/Shutterstock Images, 5 (bottom); GordanD/Shutterstock Images, 7; Savage Brothers/Wikimedia Commons, 8 (top); Dmitry Posledov/Shutterstock Images, 8 (center), 15 (top), 15 (bottom); Redwood8/Dreamstime.com, 8 (bottom), 116; Rico van Manen/Shutterstock Images, 9 (top); Warren K. Leffler/Library of Congress, 9 (center); nikshor/Shutterstock Images, 9 (bottom), 57; Westend61/Getty Images, 10; Fotokostic/Shutterstock Images, 11 (top), 81 (top); Photoongraphy/Shutterstock Images, 11 (center), 95; Claudia Harms-Warlies/Shutterstock Images, 11 (bottom); R. Gates/Staff/Getty Images, 12; Gwernol/Wikimedia Commons 13 (top); Thomas Marchhart/Shutterstock Images, 13 (bottom); 1 2 3D illustration/Shutterstock Images, 14; Trekphiler/Wikimedia Commons, 17; Alf van Beem/Wikimedia Commons, 18; Yorkshireknight/Shutterstock Images, 19; Acroterion/Wikimedia Commons, 20, 21, 90; jimflix/Flickr, 22; BulldozerD11/Tractor and Construction Plant Wiki, 23; Reise Reise/Wikimedia Commons, 24; Andy Dingley/Wikimedia Commons, 25 (top); Bettmann/Getty Images, 25 (bottom); GoUS/Alamy Stock Photo, 27; Tom Meaker/Shutterstock Images, 29, 91, 118; Different_Brian/Getty Images, 30; digitalreflections/Shutterstock Images, 31 (top); JCLobo/Shutterstock Images, 31 (bottom); Scharfsinn/Shutterstock Images, 32, 101 (bottom); maxpro/Shutterstock Images, 33 (top); Bluetoes67/Dreamstime.com, 33 (bottom); Wirestock/Getty Images, 34, 35; Ely Penner/Shutterstock Images, 36; Larry Jordan/Dreamstime.com, 37 (top); Yura Tarasovskyy/Shutterstock Images, 37 (bottom); Richard Newstead/Getty Images, 38; Loop Images/Getty Images, 39 (top); oticki/Shutterstock Images, 39 (bottom); alenvl/Shutterstock Images, 40; kallerna/Wikimedia Commons, 41 (top); katorisi/Wikimedia Commons, 41 (bottom); sheris9/Shutterstock Images, 42, 110; aleori/Shutterstock Images, 43 (top); Pressmaster/Shutterstock Images, 43 (bottom); AGCO-Fendt/Wikimedia Commons, 44; Lukasz Szwaj/Shutterstock Images, 45 (top); FreeProd33/Shutterstock Images, 45 (bottom); David M Hawthorne/Shutterstock Images, 47; Slatan/Shutterstock Images, 49; Derick P. Hudson/Shutterstock Images, 50; sunit paenphat/Shutterstock Images, 51; Kelleher Photography/Shutterstock Images, 52; Steven Cukrov/Dreamstime.com, 53 (top); Steve Cordory/Shutterstock Images, 53 (bottom); jitkagold/Shutterstock Images, 54; Matthias Mumme/Dreamstime.com, 55 (top); muri30/Getty Images, 55 (bottom); Paul J. Richards/Staff/Getty Images, 56; Richard P Long/Shutterstock Images, 59; Dan Gabriel Atanasie/Shutterstock Images, 61; Gestalt Imagery/Shutterstock Images, 62, 92, 93, 94 (top), 117; DiPres/Shutterstock Images, 63; Barry Blackburn/Dreamstime.com, 64; Brandon Woyshnis/Shutterstock Images, 65; Robert Linsdell/Wikimedia Commons, 66; Ben Birchall/PA Images/Getty Images, 67; Jaap Posthumus/Dreamstime.com, 68; SiljeAO/Shutterstock Images, 69; Karayuschij/Dreamstime.com, 70; Ballygally View Images/Shutterstock Images, 71; Rwslivka/Wikimedia Commons, 72; John Eveson/Alamy Stock Photo, 73; Wolfgang Jargstorff/Shutterstock Images, 74; Richard Semik/Shutterstock Images, 75; Jurgis Mankauskas/Shutterstock Images, 76 (top); Alexia Khruscheva/Shutterstock Images, 76 (bottom); Ruben M Ramos/Shutterstock Images, 77; Sergii_Petruk/Shutterstock Images, 78; Olexandr Panchenko/Shutterstock Images, 79 (top); Sergey Klopotov/Shutterstock Images, 79 (bottom); Yunus Simsek/Shutterstock Images, 80 (top); David Pimborough/Shutterstock Images, 80 (bottom); Veltman34/Shutterstock Images, 81 (bottom); Luce Morin/Shutterstock Images, 82; imageBROKER/Bjorn Ullhagen/Newscom, 83; Dean Clarke/Shutterstock Images, 84 (top); Peter Kniez/Shutterstock Images, 84 (bottom); vlalukinv/Shutterstock Images, 85 (top); David Calvert/Shutterstock Images, 85 (bottom); Dmitriy Kuzmichev/Shutterstock Images, 86; Andrii Yalanskyi/Getty Images, 87; Charles01/Wikimedia Commons, 88; Jason Busa/Shutterstock Images, 89; Brian Welker/Dreamstime.com, 94 (bottom); Don O'Brien/Wikimedia Commons, 96; Chuck Westerlund/Shutterstock Images, 97; Edoardo Fornaciari/Getty Images, 98; Peter Braakmann/Shutterstock Images, 99 (top); Alistair McLellan/Shutterstock Images, 99 (bottom); LivingImages/Getty Images, 100; Subitus/Shutterstock Images, 101 (top); Maksim Safaniuk/Dreamstime.com, 102; Patrick T. Fallon/Getty Images, 103; Farm Images/Getty Images, 104; Roy Hinchliffe/Dreamstime.com, 105; Alupus/Wikimedia Commons, 106 (top); volodimir bazyuk/Shutterstock Images, 106 (bottom); julie deshaies/Shutterstock Images, 107; JetKat/Shutterstock Images, 108; Piqture Kreatif/Shutterstock Images, 109; smereka/Shutterstock Images, 111 (top); Jan Toula/Shutterstock Images, 111 (bottom); Joachim Kohler Bremen/Wikimedia Commons, 112; Andrewrabbott/Wikimedia Commons, 114; Milosz Maslanka/Shutterstock Images, 115; Tonyyyy2/Wikimedia Commons, 119; Imfoto/Shutterstock Images, 120 (top); Sarah2/Dreamstime.com, 120 (bottom); carlfbagge/Wikimedia Commons, 121; Pavlo Baliukh/Shutterstock Images, 123; Vivida Photo PC/Shutterstock Images, 124 (top); astudio/Shutterstock Images, 124 (bottom); Solarisys/Shutterstock Images, 125 (top); meunierd/Shutterstock Images, 125 (bottom)